UNDERSTANDING BRITISH STRATEGIC FAILURE IN A

> The first, the supreme, the most far-reaching act of judgment that the statesman and the commander have to make is the establish ... the kind of war on which they are embarking; neither mistaking it for, nor trying to turn it into, something that is alien to its nature. This is the first of all strategic questions and the most comprehensive.[1]
>
> —Carl von Clausewitz

In the spring of 1763 the British, basking in the warm afterglow of decisive victory in the Seven Years War, presided over a vast and unprecedented global Empire. The small island nation seemingly, and rather suddenly, found itself without peer - enjoying a level of military and political hegemony not seen since the days of the Roman Empire.[2] It was a unique, albeit fleeting, position. In the span of a mere twenty years, however, the world's preeminent global power, despite enjoying a considerable advantage in almost every conceivable category used to calculate military potential, found itself disgraced and defeated by a start up nation possessing a markedly inferior *conventional* military capability. Crippled by a grossly burgeoning national debt, diplomatically isolated, and politically divided at home, Great Britain became embroiled in a protracted and unpopular global war that her policy makers and military leaders seemed incapable of understanding – much less winning – until it was far too late.[3]

The War for American Independence, especially if viewed from the British perspective, retains extraordinary significance for contemporary practitioners of national and military strategy. The conflict contains many valuable and exceedingly relevant insights regarding the rise, prevention, and challenges of insurgency, the perils of peoples' war for a foreign power, and the absolute imperative of a thoughtful, coherent, and *proactive* national strategy that integrates all instruments of national power prior to, not just after, the commencement of hostilities. The British experience also provides timeless lessons regarding the difficulties of balancing ambitious political ends with limited military means, civil-military relations, and sustaining national will in democratic societies during protracted and unpopular wars. Finally, the conflict serves as a conspicuous example of the potential for irregular warfare to thwart the application of conventionally superior military force and thereby decide or influence the political outcomes of wars and campaigns. In that regard, Great Britain's experience in the War for American Independence provides an important prologue for many of the contemporary challenges associated with the application of coercive force in a post-colonial and post-nuclear world. While predicting the future remains problematic, the United States should, in all likelihood, expect both the character and conduct of its future wars to more closely resemble that of the American Revolution, albeit from the British perspective, than those of a bygone era where industrialized nation-states waged near-total wars of annihilation.[4]

This paper uses an abbreviated examination of the Southern Campaign (1780-1782) to explore the principal causes of British strategic failure in the War for American Independence.[5] The subject demands more attention than it traditionally receives, especially from the nation that has, in the span of a mere two generations, overtaken and largely assumed Great Britain's once dominate role on the world stage. America's ascendancy, however, has not come without cost. Ironically, several of the major political, economic, and military challenges confronting the present day United States bear a remarkably similarity to those that plagued her one-time colonial master.[6] Chief among them is perhaps the most daunting and perplexing military issue of our time –

how to translate supremacy on the conventional battlefield into enduring political success in an age of austerity and limited war.

In a conflict full of dubious assumptions and missed opportunities, the pinnacle of British political and strategic miscalculation occurred in the South.[7] Though overshadowed by the dramatic events at Yorktown, the consistent and simultaneous application of *both* regular and irregular warfare during the Southern Campaign proved decisive. It, more than anything else, broke the political will of the loyalist in the region, helped wrestle control of the Southern Colonies away from the British, and contributed, in no small way, to Britain's eventual decision to abandon the war altogether. Ironically, the campaign produced no singularly decisive battle. Nor did it conform to the "traditional" view of limited dynastic warfare.[8] Instead, American success was slowly sequestered, not seized, by Major-General Nathanael Greene's astute integration of conventional and non-conventional forces in pursuit of a definitive political, not military, victory. The British, of course, made many crucial errors. Whether the Americans won the Southern Campaign or the British lost it remains an intriguing historical question significantly beyond the scope of this paper. Greene, and his fellow Patriots, however, realized what a host of British commanders and their political masters in Whitehall could not - the war in the south, like the Revolution itself, was a complex, unconventional, and violent political struggle for the loyalty and allegiance of the American population writ large. It could not, and would not, be decided by the application of conventional military force alone.[9]

The Devolution of British Strategy

In December of 1774, a presumptuous King George III boldly asserted, "The New England governments are in a State of Rebellion. *Blows must decide* whether they are to be subject to this country or independent."[10] With the clairvoyance of hindsight, however, the British decision to employ force in the spring of 1775 rested on two fundamental miscalculations. First, the authorities in London, both civilian and military, underestimated the fighting qualities and martial prowess of the American militia.[11] Second, most, if not all, of these same men, severely misjudged the extent and veracity of popular support the Patriot cause enjoyed, not just in New England, but throughout the thirteen colonies.[12] Fiscal and political constraints in London demanded a quick and efficient termination of the conflict in America. An emphasis on the former, however, precluded a realistic and prescient understanding of the latter. The result was an overly sanguine view of the *actual* political situation in the colonies and the adoption of a British military strategy that, though it considered the alternative of a naval war, remained wedded to the promise of decisive battle until the twin disasters of Saratoga and the subsequent signing of the Franco-American alliance in February 1778 forced a dramatic reordering of priorities.[13]

The Americans, too, initially miscalculated. The wave of revolutionary enthusiasm that crested with the British evacuation of Boston and signing of the Declaration of Independence gave way to the harsh reality of Washington's near destruction at New York and the stark realization that "native courage" and revolutionary zeal, alone, could not secure independence.[14] Unlike his British counterparts, however, Washington demonstrated considerable pragmatism in the face of necessity.[15] Although he longed for a "conventional" victory against British regulars, by September 1776 Washington curtailed his initial strategic designs in favor of a Fabian approach focused on the enduring political, not military, objective: "We should on all occasions avoid a general action, and put nothing to risk unless compelled by a necessity, into which we ought never to be drawn."[16]

The British never fully reconciled their faith in decisive battle with the fact that Washington, after barely escaping from New York in the fall of 1776, had no intention of giving it. Deeply flawed strategic assumptions combined with chance, the tyranny of distance in the age of sail, and episodes of tactical blundering precluded the destruction of Washington's fledgling continental army and led to the unconscionable surrender of General John Burgoyne's entire command at Saratoga in the fall of 1777.[17] Worse, France's formal entry into the war in March 1778 transformed the suppression of an internal rebellion into a global conflict.[18] Suddenly, Great Britain, for the first time in 150 years, found herself without the aid or support of a single continental ally while engaged in a dangerous and rapidly escalating war with her ancient Bourbon rivals.[19] Operations in America, particularly for the Admiralty, became secondary to defense of the British Isles and larger economic interests in the Caribbean. Accordingly, in the spring of 1778, the North Ministry assumed a defensive posture in America.[20] Diplomatically isolated and forced to react to the imminent threat of French sea power, the government recalled its Commander-in-Chief in America, Major-General William Howe, ordered the evacuation of Philadelphia, and grudgingly dispatched the Earle of Carlisle on a desperate, and poorly timed, attempt to secure peace with honor in the colonies.[21]

By the close of 1779, however, it became increasingly clear that Great Britain, despite an enormous expenditure of blood and treasure, was losing the war.[22] The revolutionaries maintained tenuous, but effective, control over the vast majority of the colonial population. British forces, by contrast, found themselves confined to the coastal enclaves of New York, Long Island, and Savannah, under the constant and very real threat of a menacing French fleet. More importantly, four years of military paralysis, France's entry into the war, and a steadily deteriorating strategic situation emboldened a vocal and increasingly effective **political opposition** in the House of Commons.[23] The 1778 naval crisis followed by Admiral Keppel's court martial, the failure of the Carlisle Peace Commission, and the raucous parliamentary inquiry into Sir William Howe's generalship produced a series of inimical public debates that exposed, for all to see, a pattern of ministerial blundering and an ominous break down in civil-military relations.[24] The events cast a long shadow on the government's planning and conduct of the war and unleashed a torrent of political blame and recrimination that very nearly toppled the North Ministry.[25]

    The government's tenuous and slowly eroding support in Parliament, forced a tacit reversal of military policy. Only by insisting that the war for America could still be won, not with an endless and expensive supply of reinforcements buttressing a failed strategy, but rather by harnessing dormant loyalist strength to champion a new one, could the Ministry maintain the requisite political support to continue the war.[26] The idea exploited long-standing, though increasingly questionable, assumptions about loyalist strength in the south and conveniently nested with the government's plans to shift the seat of the war to the Caribbean.[27] In December of 1779, Howe's successor, Lieutenant-General Henry Clinton embarked the majority of his army in New York harbor and sailed for Charleston, long viewed as the key to political control of the southern colonies and an important port for future operations in the West Indies. The seizure of Charleston, intended to relieve pressure on loyalist forces operating in Georgia, also constituted the initial phase of a larger "southern strategy" designed to ignite a counter-revolution in the Carolinas by reestablishing royal government and recruiting loyalist militia, supported by a small number of British regulars, to defend it.[28] In many ways, the belated adaptation of a "pacification" strategy, conceived in the caldron of wartime domestic politics vice the crucible of deliberate military design, represented Britain's last best hope.[29] Unfortunately for the British cause, it became bungled in execution by an increasingly dysfunctional Ministry that continued to see and hear what conformed to its concerted view and a bold and audacious commander who stubbornly clung to the chimera of decisive battle until it was far too late.[30]

The Seizure of Charleston

On February 1, 1780, a powerful expeditionary force under the command of Sir Henry Clinton landed on Simmons Island, thirty miles south of Charleston. By late March, Clinton, with approximately 12,000 troops, crossed the Ashley River and laid siege to the beleaguered city. Isolated and cut off, Major General Benjamin Lincoln reluctantly surrendered the city and its 5,500 defenders on May 12. The disaster at Charleston, by far the greatest calamity to befall any American army during the war, emboldened the loyalists and nearly broke the back of the Patriot cause in South Carolina. Clinton moved quickly to restore British authority. He organized provincial militia units and initially implemented a liberal pacification policy, whereby the majority of former Patriots were paroled and allowed to return to their homes.[31]

By late May, however, Clinton and his naval counterpart, Admiral Mariot Arbuthnot, became increasingly concerned over reports of a French fleet headed for North America. As they hastily re-embarked for New York to counter the threat, the British Commander-in-Chief, still exultant in the wake of his stunning success at Charleston, made a fateful decision. Realizing his pending departure would dramatically reduce British troop strength in the Carolinas and that the benevolence of the crown's original parole policies precluded the recruitment of enough locally raised provincial militia to make up the difference, Clinton suddenly reversed himself. On June 3, he issued a new proclamation forcing paroled former Patriots to swear an oath of allegiance to the King and, more importantly, to actively engage in supporting royal authority. The decision, born out of practical military necessity, constituted a grievous political miscalculation.[32] While it was reasonable to expect a former Whig to give up the fight and return home, it was quite another matter to now force him to take up arms against his friends and neighbors.

Victory Was Never Enough

Cornwallis assumed command of the Southern Army on June 5. He wasted little time implementing Clinton's new policy and expanding British control over the region. With his seaboard bases at Savannah, Beaufort, Charleston, and Georgetown now secure, Cornwallis aggressively projected British expeditionary power deep into the country's interior. He established a series of garrisons along the Saluda River westward to Ninety-Six and pursued the scattered remnants of the Continental army north along the Catawba River valley. On August 16, Cornwallis, with just 2,200 troops, shattered General Horatio Gates at Camden and sent what remained of the demoralized American army scurrying across the North Carolina border toward Charlotte. Ironically, though no organized Continental force remained in the Carolinas, the seeds of political disaster, long ignored or completely misunderstood, now sprouted in the wake of Cornwallis's conventional success.[33]

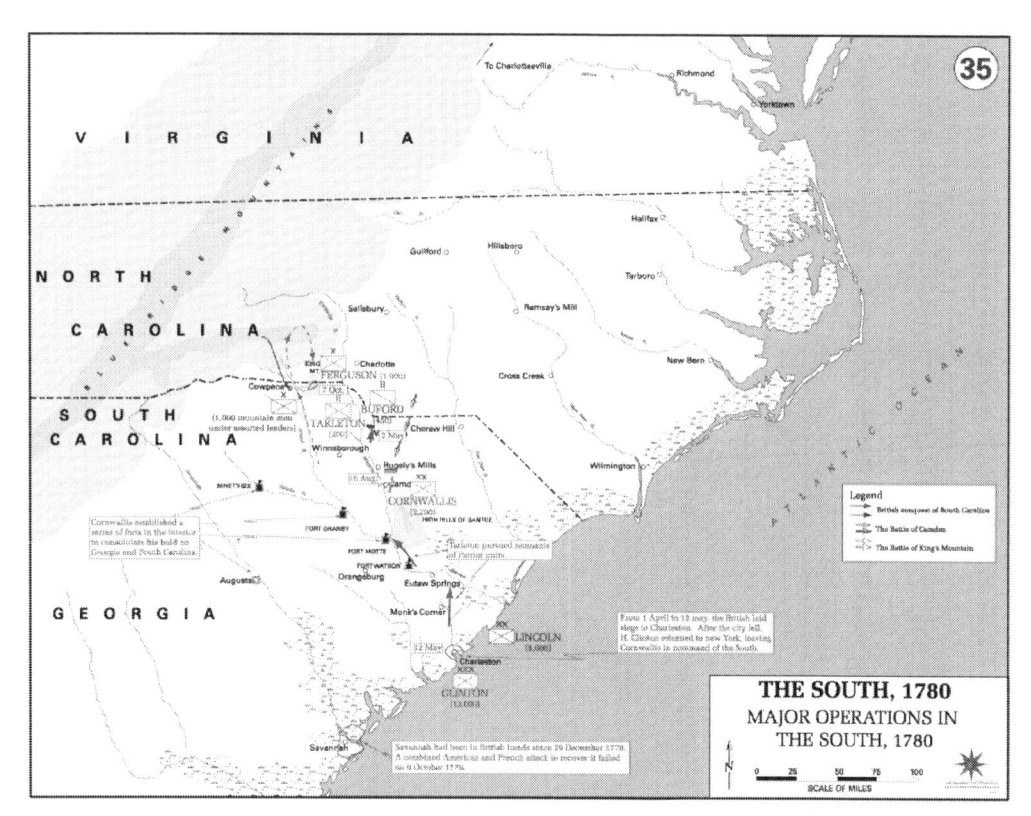

Figure 1: Cornwallis's Operations in 1780[34]

Cornwallis's army, even with the addition of a substantial number of loyalist militia, was simply too small to consolidate British authority over so large an area. Moreover, the combination of imperial hubris and the flawed implementation of Clinton's pacification policies ignited an insurgency that quickly metastasized into a ruthless and bloody civil war.[35] American guerrillas led by Thomas Sumter, Francis Marion, and Andrew Pickens attacked British outposts and threatened lines of communications.[36] More significantly, while Cornwallis and his loyalist militia searched in vain for the remnants of Gates scattered Continentals far to the north, American partisans killed or intimidated large numbers of Tories, who suddenly found themselves outnumbered and unprotected.[37]

On October 7, a motley collection of rugged American mountain men destroyed one of Cornwallis's flanking columns, under the command of Major Patrick Ferguson, at Kings Mountain. The Scotch-Irish Presbyterians of the Watauga region established a semi- autonomous community in the mountains of western North Carolina after the Battle of Alamance in 1771.[38] They harbored no particular loyalty to either crown or the fledgling United States, but watched with increasing trepidation as Ferguson's column, comprised entirely of loyalist militia, approached their homes. When the impetuous British Major threatened to "burn the whole country" if the frontiersmen did not turn over the Patriot Colonel Isaac Shelby, known to be taking refuge in the area, over a thousand back woods riflemen emerged out of nowhere and quickly overwhelmed the column.[39] The British lost 1,125 men in the hour-long battle, including at least nine prominent Tories who were hastily tried and summarily executed. Kings Mountain marked a significant turning point in the war. The shocking reversal all but destroyed the loyalist movement in the region and forced a stunned Cornwallis, then on the outskirts of Charlotte, to beat a hasty retreat south into the Palmetto State.[40]

The Road to Guilford Courthouse

Nathanael Greene arrived in Charlotte on December 2, 1780. The former Quaker turned Patriot inherited less than fifteen hundred disorganized and dispirited men.[41] Upon his selection to replace Gates as the commander of the Southern Department, Greene undertook a detailed study of the topography and terrain of the region. He harbored no illusions, however, about the dismal prospects of defeating Cornwallis in a conventional military campaign. As such, Greene proposed "to equip a flying army of about eight hundred horse and one thousand infantry… and make a kind of partisan war."[42] On December 4, he established communications with Francis Marion and other partisan leaders. Greene encouraged cooperation and implored Patriot irregulars to provide intelligence and continue their subversive operations, while he made plans and preparations to regain the initiative.[43]

In late December, Greene moved south and boldly divided his army in the face of Cornwallis's superior force. On January 17, Greene's western detachment, commanded by Daniel Morgan, bated Lieutenant-Colonel Banastre Tarleton into giving battle at Cowpens.[44] The subsequent destruction of a second isolated British column in less than four months incensed Cornwallis, but did little to alter his thinking regarding the utility of conventional military force in a peoples' war. As Patriot militiamen simply melted back into the countryside, the enraged British general initiated an ill-advised and impetuous pursuit of Morgan that took him across the border and deep into western North Carolina.

Greene hastened north and consolidated his rag tag army, but refused to give battle. On January 26, a frustrated Cornwallis, now operating over extended lines of communications and unable to catch the fleet footed Americans, decided to burn his army's baggage.[45] The move did little to improve his mobility relative to the Americans. Greene continued a cat and mouse game of provocation luring the British further north, while his partisans and militia continued to harass British foraging parties and communications. On March 15, Greene, his ranks temporarily buoyed by an influx of militia, finally gave battle at Guilford Court House. The British held the field, but it was a classic pyrrhic victory. Over a quarter of Cornwallis's army lay dead or wounded.[46] Running dangerously low on supplies and realizing that another "victory" over Greene would destroy his emaciated army, Cornwallis left seventy of his most seriously wounded in a Quaker meeting house at New Garden, reluctantly turned his back on the Piedmont, and marched to the sea.[47]

The paucity of loyalist support, not logistical difficulties, proved decisive in Cornwallis's fateful decision to abandon the Carolinas. Throughout the campaign,

Cornwallis stubbornly clung to the belief that a decisive tactical victory over Greene would liberate or somehow empower the crown's many loyalist friends to join him. Guilford Court House finally shattered his naivety. Reflecting on the indecisive nature of the campaign, a frustrated Cornwallis observed, "Many rode into camp, shook me by the hand, said they were glad to see us, and that we had beat Greene, then rode home again. I could not get a hundred men in all the Regulator's country to stay with us even as militia." [48]

Cornwallis's army limped into Wilmington on April 7. Three days later, the dejected general wrote to Clinton in New York, "I cannot help but expressing my wishes that the Chesapeake may become the seat of the war." [49] Amazingly, even at this late hour, Cornwallis still thought "a successful battle may give us America." [50] Greene, however, did not wait idle as the British contemplated shifting operations to Virginia. On March 29, he decided to "carry the war immediately into South Carolina." [51] As Cornwallis moved north toward his rendezvous with destiny, Greene and his American partisans returned to the very seat of British power in the South. Unlike Cornwallis, however, Greene's objectives were political not military. Though he continued to lose battles, Hobkirk's Hill on April 25 and Eutaw Springs on September 8, he nonetheless succeeded in further eroding British authority and political support amongst the people of South Carolina. One by one, isolated British outposts scattered throughout the interior fell to Greene and his partisans. By October the tide of British expeditionary power that had once stretched to the mountains of western North Carolina receded to the coastal bastions of Charleston and Savannah.[52]

Defeat by Indecision

When the unfathomable news of Yorktown reached London in November 1781, the American Secretary, Lord George Germain, grasping for the straws of an increasingly unlikely military victory, proposed raising a force of 28,000 men to hold the coastal enclaves of New York, Charleston, and Savanna.[53] Similarly, in late December, the Governor of New York, James Robertson, pleaded for reinforcements and the resumption of offensive warfare in the north, arguing that "an army without hope of getting back America should not stay in it."[54] Unfortunately for the North Ministry and the thousands of Loyalists in America it was the Governor's tacit admission, not his call for still more troops in support of an expensive and increasingly desultory war, which more accurately reflected the political reality of a deeply divided Great Britain.[55] Germain, long buffeted by an angry sea of political recrimination, finally resigned in early February. His replacement, Welbore Ellis, addressed a skeptical Parliament on 22 February in a desperate attempt to rally the fragile and rapidly eroding political support for the Kings policies. Remarkably, the Ministry, rekindling the strategic debate after the Saratoga disaster, now adopted a subtle variation of the opposition's long-standing argument against continuation of the war.

> As to the American war, it had always been his firm opinion, that it was just in its origin… but he never entertained an idea, nor did he believe any man in that House ever imagined, that America was to be reduced to obedience by force; his ideal always was that in America we had many friends; and by strongly supporting them, we should be able to destroy that party or faction that wished for war… To destroy that faction, and assist our friends there in that desired object, was, in his opinion, the true and only object of the war. Whether that object was now attainable, was the matter…to be considered.[56]

The opposition, vindicated by the Ministry's tacit admission of failure and galvanized by a rapid and unprecedented influx of political defections, decided it was not. On 27 February, the House of Commons formally denounced "the further prosecution of offensive warfare on the continent of North America, for the purpose of reducing the revolted colonies to obedience by force."[57] Less than a month later, the

North Ministry collapsed under the weight of a protracted, unpopular, and, in the minds of most Englishmen, an ill-advised, poorly planned, and increasingly unwinnable war.[58] On 27 March, the King, after briefly contemplating abdication, begrudgingly turned to the opposition who formed a new government under the leadership of the Marquis of Rockingham. The new Ministry quickly abolished the American Department and ordered the evacuation of New York, Charleston, and Savannah.[59] In the process, the Rockingham Ministry accomplished what Washington's intrepid army, even after it was augmented by powerful French expeditionary forces and buoyed by the British disaster at Yorktown, could never do – it physically removed the world's dominant military power from America.

War Turned Upside Down

Insurgencies represent complex political, social, and military problems. They require an adroit, sophisticated, and flexible integration of all instruments of national power to defeat or prevent. It would be wrong to pin the crown's failure in the South on Cornwallis alone, for the seeds of the British disaster in America lay deep and were sown many years prior by men occupying more influential positions.[60] Yet, Cornwallis, like the vast majority of his British colleagues, fundamentally misunderstood both the nature and the character of the war in the South. He embarked upon an ill-conceived and tragically flawed campaign that focused, almost exclusively, on the physical destruction of an enemy army. Moreover, Cornwallis's tactical and operational plans, while bold and audacious, were not in consonance with the spirit or intent of Clinton's instructions or the shift in British strategy made necessary by France's entry into the war.[61] The Americans, by contrast, employed a decentralized strategy that concentrated, not on the annihilation of British military forces, but rather at securing the political and popular support of the indigenous population.[62]

Throughout the campaign the British consistently overestimated both the extent and capabilities of loyalist support, failed to secure the local population, and seemed incapable of comprehending that the loyalty of the people trumped the quest for tactical glories.[63] The destruction of unsupported Tory units at Ramsour's Mill, North Carolina and King's Mountain, South Carolina in 1780 stifled the further recruitment of fence sitters and sent a chilling message to would be loyalists. Though a significant percentage of the population were indifferent or actually harbored pro-British sentiment, Cornwallis, by and large, failed to secure it.[64] Marauding Southern partisans prosecuted a shadowing, but effective, campaign of fear and intimidation that eventually cemented the loyalties and allegiance of population.[65] Ironically, Cornwallis facilitated Patriot political success by impetuously chasing Gates, and then Greene, into the strategically insignificant terrain of the mountainous southern back country and implementing flawed political-military policies that led to repressive acts of violence against the civil population under British control.[66]

Greene and the Americans, by contrast, owed their success to the confluence of three principal factors. First, the terrain in the Carolinas, both human and physical, facilitated Patriot operations.[67] The region's ambiguous political loyalties, restricted mobility, and challenging topography all leant themselves to the type of isolated, hit and run, small unit tactics employed by Greene and his partisans. Second, Greene's sophisticated comprehension of the relationship between military means and political ends precluded the destruction of his undermanned army, fueled the insurgency, and ultimately consummated his military endeavors with enduring political success. Lacking in tactical acumen, he nonetheless proved patient and pragmatic. He only gave battle when he knew he could win or when the political or strategic gains clearly exceeded the tactical price.[68] Finally, the tenacity and fighting qualities of the Southern partisan proved decisive. The Patriot cause inherited an exceptional cadre of experienced and committed irregulars. Thomas Sumter, William Moultrie, Francis Marion, Issac Huger, and Andrew Pickens organized and led small, but highly effective, partisan units. These men, all veteran Indian fighters, possessed in depth knowledge of the local terrain and had long ago mastered the unconventional methods of irregular warfare. For many, including both Sumter and Pickens, their visceral hatred of the British cemented their loyalty to the Patriot cause and insured that there would be no turning back.[69]

The war in the South was not won or lost on the conventional battlefield. American success was the product of a complex, unconventional, and violent political struggle for the loyalty and allegiance of the southern population. American partisans, operating in countless towns and villages and employing methods of political coercion that would appear unconscionable to us today, proved decisive. While it seems unlikely that a man of Greene's Quaker upbringing would have openly condoned these draconian tactics, many of which bear a striking similarity to the abhorrent, but nonetheless, classic, insurgent tactics used in Algeria, Vietnam, and Iraq, he most certainly knew they were being employed. Not long after his arrival in the South he noted with a considerable degree of resignation:

> There is not a day passes but there are more or less who fall a sacrifice to this savage disposition. The Whigs seem determined to extirpate the Tories and the Tories the Whigs.... If a stop cannot be put to these massacres, the country will be depopulated... as neither Whig nor Tory can live.[70]

Operating over a century and a half prior to Mao, Greene and his partisan collogues mastered the quintessential elements of guerrilla warfare. He possessed the presence of mind and clairvoyance of thought to employ a hybrid combination of conventional and non-conventional methods in pursuit of a decisive political, not military, outcome. Greene realized, through a strange combination of necessity and serendipity, what Cornwallis could not - the Southern Revolution was a violent internal political struggle between the Tories and Whigs of the Carolinas. It may be doubted today, with a considerable degree of legitimacy, whether the British, burdened with the global responsibilities of empire and shackled by the tyranny of distance in the age of sail, could have ever prevailed in the face of such a complicated and unconventional undertaking.[71] It appears certain, however, that the conflict in the South constituted a type of warfare that Cornwallis and his political masters in London were unprepared to confront and, most assuredly, failed to comprehend until it was far too late.[72]

Conclusion: The Futility of Force and the Preservation of Power

Admittedly, the selective use of history is dangerous, but a careful examination of the principal causes of British strategic failure in America offers a series of profound lessons for the exercise and preservation of U.S. national power in an age of austerity and limited war.[73] First, an overreliance on tactical prowess, manifested in the false hope of decisive battle, constitutes a poor substitute for a thoughtful, coherent, and *proactive* national strategy that integrates all instruments of national power prior to, not just after, the commencement of hostilities. Great Britain, not unlike the modern United States, was a seafaring nation not a dominant land power. Endowed with the blessings of geography, the United Kingdom traditionally exercised strategic patience combined with sea power, economic leverage, and forward thinking diplomacy to compensate for the inherent limitations of its ground forces.[74] All three of these enlightened and far-sighted national policies failed or were never fully developed during the War for American Independence.[75]

Once hostilities commenced, the British government consistently struggled to achieve unity of effort across a compartmentalized and non-integrated ministerial system. The fragmented nature of the imperial bureaucracy eventually resulted in an increase in the power and influence of the American Department. This did not, however, insure cross-departmental integration or the development of a prescient national strategy to deal with the problem of rebellion.[76] Britain's senior military officer, Adjutant-General Thomas Harvey railed at the prospect of using the British Army to subdue America, "it is impossible to conquer it with our British Army… To attempt to conquer it internally by our land force is as wild an idea as ever controverted common sense."[77] Harvey was not alone. While most officials in the British government agreed that force could be used, there was considerable divergence of opinion on whether it should be.[78] Similarly, many senior political and military leaders advocated a maritime strategy based on economic pressure and British sea power, believing the rebellion would eventually fall under its own weight.[79]

Such sage political-military advice, however, fell on deaf ears, hijacked, in large measure, by the vocal remonstrations of several Colonial Governors who fueled the false belief that the rebellion was the work of a vocal minority of "turbulent and seditious" individual political agitators.[80] Similarly, several influential ministers advanced equally irresponsible myths of martial superiority. Sir Jeffery Amherst, for one, boasted that he could, with just 5,000 men, sweep from one end of America to another.

Likewise, Lord Sandwich of the Admiralty declared that the Americans would run at "the very sound of cannon…as fast as their feet could carry them."[81] The North ministry eventually turned, despite the warnings of its senior officer in America, General Thomas Gage, to the one element of national power it could control and employ in short order – the military.[82] In retrospect, it could legitimately be argued, that Great Britain's strategic leaders lost the War for America before it ever began.[83]

The British experience with irregular warfare, particularly in the South, constitutes a second and exceedingly relevant lesson for the contemporary United States. The American Revolution differed significantly from the traditional dynastic wars of the eighteenth-century.[84] Though there were compelling elements of the later that gave the conflict an appearance of conventional interstate warfare, in reality, a loose confederation of Patriot militia and political leaders, cementing the loyalty and allegiance of their fellow countrymen in countless towns and villages, not the application of regular military force, proved decisive. An important, if generally underappreciated, phenomenon clearly articulated by the late Walter Mills:

> Repeatedly it was the militia which met the critical emergency or, in less formal operations, kept control of the country, cut off foragers, captured British agents, intimidated the war-weary and disaffected or tarred and feathered the notorious Tories. While the regular armies marched and fought more or less ineffectually, it was the militia which presented the greatest single impediment to Britain's only practicable weapon, that of counter-revolution.[85]

Britain's army, like that of the modern Unites States, was trained, organized, and equipped to seek decisive battle, with a like opponent, operating under the traditional political-military construct of the Clausewitzian trinity.[86] This paradigm, while applicable in conventional interstate conflict, proved woefully inadequate for the challenges and nuance of intra-state warfare waged against an extra-legal political entity.[87] While British tactical acumen proved effective militarily, it could never, in and of itself, secure the loyalty or allegiance of the population. The creation of numerous provincial units like the Queens Rangers, Tarleton's Legion, et al. reinforces the idea that several British tactical and operational commanders, over time, came to appreciate the reality and the complexities of the type of war upon which they were engaged.[88] The development of British strategy, however, struggled to catch up to the facts on the ground.[89] Ultimately, the British Army, not unlike the employment of U.S. forces in Vietnam, proved neither an adequate shield for the loyalist population nor a terrible swift-sword capable of destroying a fledgling, but increasingly capable, Continental Army and thus in waging a war it was not intellectually prepared to fight, the British Army lost the opportunity to fight the war it knew how to win.[90]

Finally, British strategic failure in America serves as a powerful reminder that the long-term interest of the state must not fall victim to fear, honor, and an overinflated view of what is militarily possible or wise.[91] Throughout the war the British, "made their plans to suit their understanding of the rebellion and that understanding was shaped consistently by ignorance and by wishful thinking."[92] America can ill afford to be provoked or deluded into making a similar mistake in the twenty-first century.[93] A great nation, to remain so, must employ superior strategic thinking and foresight to avoid the perils of desultory warfare or the necessity to exercise superior force in the first place. The tragedy for the United States is not that it lost the Vietnam War or now finds itself mired in two expensive, protracted, and irregular conflicts in Iraq and Afghanistan, but rather, in the process of usurping Great Britain as the economic, political, and military leader of the free world it seemingly forgot a series of lessons that it once taught.[94]

British strategic failure in America, not unlike the French in Algeria, the United States in Vietnam, or the Soviets in Afghanistan, demonstrated the futility of limited *conventional* military force to solve what was essentially a political problem and terminated, only belatedly, with a somber realization that the country's long-term interest demanded the preservation of her national power, vice the short-term and perpetual expenditure of it, in pursuit of a political objective that was in no way commensurate with the costs.[95] Unwilling to destroy the colonies in order to save them, British military strategy became a reluctant prisoner of deeply flawed strategic assumptions, a government that failed to determine a realistic and militarily attainable political objective, and a blatant inability to accurately determine the kind of war upon which the nation was engaged until it was far too late.

Viewed in this light, the Southern Campaign, represents not so much the separate and distinct phase of the war it is so often portrayed to be, but rather, reflected the logical byproduct of years of political miscalculation and the devolution of a military strategy that increasingly came to rely on a "pacification" strategy, predicated on the promise of loyalist support, to compensate for a paucity of both troops and political will to continue a controversial, expensive, and increasing unpopular war. It also represented a belated, though certainly unstated, admission that *blows* alone, or more precisely, the chimera of decisive battle, could not secure the loyalty and allegiance of an ambivalent or hostile people, numerous, and armed. In the process, the British learned that battlefield brilliance seldom rescues bad strategy, there are, in fact, limits to what military force can achieve, and national leaders who base their plans and policies primarily on hope and a stubborn belief in the sanctity of their own concerted views, if wrong, can lead a nation to disaster. We should not hold the British in contempt nor hypocritically criticize their strategic failure in America; we should learn from it - *ex preteritus nostrum posterus.*

Endnotes

[1] Carl Von Clausewitz, *On War,* Michael Howard and Peter Paret, eds. (Princeton: The Princeton University Press, 1976), 88-89.

[2] For perspective on both the extent and challenges associated with precipitous rise of British hegemony in the wake of the Seven Years War see, Fred Anderson, *Crucible of War: The Seven Years' War and the Fate of Empire in British North America, 1754-1766* (New York: Alfred A. Knopf, 2000), 503-506, 516-517 and Brendan Simms, *Three Victories and a Defeat: The Rise and Fall of the First British Empire, 1714-1783* (New York: Basic Books, 2007), 501-531.

[3] John Brewer, *The Sinews of Power: War, Money and the English State, 1688-1783* (London: Unwin Hyman, 1989), 115. Fiscal pressures played a significant, if generally underappreciated, role in both the cause and termination of the War for American Independence. Great Britain's national debt nearly doubled during the Seven Years War rising from 80 million pounds at the commencement of hostilities to 140 million pounds in 1763. Similarly, during the War for American Independence the national debt exploded from 130 million pounds in 1775 to nearly 240 million pounds by 1783.

[4] The apparent impracticality of high-intensity "conventional" warfare is briefly addressed in Rupert Smith's, *The Utility of Force: The Art of War in the Modern World.* (London: Allen Lane, 2005), 269-307. For broader perspective on the evolution of warfare see, Archer Jones, *The Art of War in the Western World* (London: Harrap, 1988); Theodore Ropp, *War in the Modern World* (New York: Collier Books, 1962); J.F.C. Fuller's, *The Conduct of War, 1789-1961; A Study of the Impact of the French, Industrial, and Russian Revolutions on War and its Conduct* (New Brunswick, N.J.: Rutgers University Press, 1961) and *A Military History of the Western World* (New York: Funk & Wagnalls, 1954). In many ways the evolution of warfare could be seen as unwinding in the aftermath of the apogee of the Second World War and the introduction of nuclear weapons. One only need look at the decidedly mixed record of conventionally superior forces in the post-World War II era for evidence of this counterintuitive phenomenon. It appears that "traditional" warfare between nation states has receded to something more akin to the limited, dynastic, conflicts that characterized the eighteenth-century vice the industrialized, near total, wars of annihilation that marked the twentieth-century. The apparent decoupling of traditional military force with the ability to achieve enduring political success is a function of an increasingly proliferated, politically complex, and globally integrated world. These trends will likely accelerate in the years ahead.

[5] William B. Wilcox, *Portrait of a General; Sir Henry Clinton in the War of Independence* (New York, Knopf; 1964), vii.

[6] John D. Hayes, "Lessons from British History," *Military Affairs* 17, no. 3 (Autumn, 1953): 137-140. Hayes's persuasive and well written essay argues, "Great Britain has been our precursor in many ways. World power and control of the seas are the more evident. Some Toynbee of the XXV century may interpret the establishment of the United States as a major step in the great English speaking democratic evolution, a historical process as evident then as the Greco-Roman and the Hebraic pictures are to us now. Whatever may be the merits of such historical theorizing, it is a historical fact that British problems of the past are strikingly similar to ours today. Control of the seas, industrial power, financial strength, leadership in opposition to totalitarianism in all its forms, - in each of these roles the United States has become heir within two generations." For a similar, if slightly expanded, version of the argument see, Niall Ferguson, *Empire the Rise and Demise of the British World Order and the Lessons for Global Power* (New York: Basic Books, 2003), 303-317.

[7] British military and political blundering constitutes a pervasive and powerful theme throughout the historiography. See for example, William Seymour and W. F. N. Watson, *The Price of Folly: British Blunders in the War of American Independence*. (London: Brassey's, 1995) and Don Cook's, *The Long Fuse: How England Lost the American Colonies, 1760-1785* (New York: Atlantic Monthly Press, 1995). For succinct overviews of the flawed strategic thinking contributing to two of the most prominent British military disasters of the war see William B. Wilcox, "Too Many Cooks: British Planning before Saratoga," *Journal of British Studies* 2, no. 1 (Nov., 1962): 56-90 and "The British Road to Yorktown: A Study in Divided Command," *The American Historical Review* 52, no. 1 (Oct., 1946): 1-35. Paul H. Smith's, *Loyalists and Redcoats: A Study in British Revolutionary Policy* (Chapel Hill: University of North Carolina Press, 1964) emphasizes the fateful consequences of Whitehall's consistent and blatant misreading of both the strength and capabilities of loyalist support throughout the war. John Shy's classic, *Toward Lexington; The Role of the British Army in the Coming of the American Revolution* (Princeton, N.J.: Princeton University Press, 1965) examines the causes and consequences of permanently garrisoning British regulars in North America in the aftermath of the Seven Years War. Robert W. Tucker and David C. Hendrickson's, *The Fall of the First British Empire: Origins of the War of American Independence* (Baltimore: Johns Hopkins University Press, 1982) offers a sympathetic interpretation of the numerous fiscal and political policies that contributed to the outbreak of hostilities. Arthur Bowler's, *Logistics and the Failure of the British Army in America, 1775-1783* (Princeton, N.J.: Princeton University Press, 1975) places the problems of British military strategy and operations within the larger context of logistics and the tyranny of distance in the age of sail.

[8] Allan Millett and Peter Maslowski, *For the Common Defense: A Military History of the United States of America*. (New York: Free Press, 1984), 51. For greater perspective on the age of limited dynastic warfare see, JFC Fuller's, *The Conduct of War, 1789-1961; A Study of the Impact of the French, Industrial, and Russian Revolutions on War and its Conduct* (New Brunswick, N.J.: Rutgers University Press, 1961), 21-25 and Theodore Ropp, *War in the Modern World* (New York: Collier Books, 1962), 19-53.

[9] The author's views and interpretations on the irregular character of the Southern Campaign remain heavily influenced by Jac Weller, "Irregular but Effective: Partisan Weapons Tactics in the American Revolution, Southern Theatre," *Military Affairs* 21, no. 3 (Autumn, 1957): 118-131 and "The Irregular War in the South," *Military Affairs* 24, no. 3, Irregular Warfare Issue (Autumn, 1960): 124-136. Also see, Robert Pugh, "The Revolutionary Militia in the Southern Campaign, 1780-1781," *The William and Mary Quarterly* 14, no. 2 (Apr., 1957): 154-175 and John Shy, "A New Look at Colonial Militia," *The William and Mary Quarterly* 20, no. 2 (April,

1963): 175-185. The most important secondary sources emphasizing the irregular character of the Southern Campaign remain Russell Weigley's, *The Partisan War: The South Carolina Campaign of 1780-1782* (Columbia: University of South Carolina Press, 1970) and John Morgan Dederer's, *Making Bricks Without Straw: Nathanael Greene's Southern Campaign and Mao Tse-Tung's Mobile War* (Manhattan, Kan., USA: Sunflower University Press, 1983) which constitutes an in depth expansion of his original article "Making Bricks without Straw: Nathanael Greene's Southern Campaigns and Mao Tse-Tung's Mobile War," *Military Affairs* 47, no. 3 (Oct., 1983): 115-121. Don Higginbotham, *The War of American Independence; Military Attitudes, Policies, and Practice, 1763-1789* (New York: Macmillan, 1971) remains the best single volume military history of the conflict. For a succinct analysis of the Southern Campaign within the larger context of the war see pp. 352-388.

[10] King George III to Lord North, December 1774, quoted in Cook, *The Long Fuse*, 200.

[11] Higginbotham, *The War of American Independence*, 51-52. These attitudes were largely based on British observations of American militia's performance during the French and Indian War. For additional perspectives on British military attitudes towards America see Stephen Conway, "To Subdue America: British Army Officers and the Conduct of the Revolutionary War," *The William and Mary Quarterly* 43, no. 3 (Jul., 1986): 381-407 and Peter E. Russell, "Redcoats in the Wilderness: British Officers and Irregular Warfare in Europe and America, 1740 to 1760," *The William and Mary Quarterly* 35, no. 4 (Oct., 1978): 629-652.

[12] The theme pervades the literature. See for example, Higginbotham, *The War of American Independence*, 51-52; Millett and Maslowski, *For the Common Defense*, 51-52; Shy, *A People Numerous and Armed*, 81-116 and 222-225; and Piers Mackesy, *The War for America, 1775-1783* (Cambridge: Harvard University Press, 1964), 36. For more on General Gage's political and military estimates of the situation and his role in the conflict see John Richard Alden's, *General Gage in America* Baton Rouge (Louisiana State University Press, 1948), 218-232 and "Why the March to Concord?," *The American Historical Review* 49, no. 3 (Apr., 1944): 446-454. Also see John Shy, "Thomas Gage: Weak Link of Empire," in George A. Billias, ed., *George Washington's Opponents: British Generals and Admirals in the American Revolution* (New York, 1969), 24-27.

[13] For perspective on the development of British military strategy see Jeremy Black, *War for America: The Fight for Independence, 1775-1783* (New York: St. Martin's Press, 1991), 13-40; Mackesy, *The War for America*, 27-40; and Ira Gruber's "The Origins of British Strategy in the War for American Independence," in Stanley J. Underal ed., *Military History of the American Revolution* (Washington, DC: Office of Air Force History, 1976), 38-64.

[14] Charles Royster, *A Revolutionary People At War: The Continental Army and American Character, 1775-1783* (Chapel Hill: The University of North Carolina Press, 1996), 58-96.

[15] David R. Palmer, "American Strategy Reconsidered," in Stanley J. Underal ed., *Military History of the American Revolution* (Washington, DC: Office of Air Force History, 1976), 52-64. Palmer emphasized Washington's pragmatism and strategic patience in the face of necessity. He argued that Washington, throughout what he identified as three separate and distinct stages or phases of the conflict, specifically tailored his strategy to the political/military situation at hand vice falling victim to dogma. The argument is fully developed in Palmer's, *The Way of the Fox; American Strategy in the War for America, 1775-1783* (Westport, Conn.: Greenwood Press, 1975), 200-204.

[16] Washington to Congress, 8 September, 1776. John C. Fitzpatrick ed., *The Writings of George Washington from the Original Manuscript Sources 1745-1799* (Westport, Conn.: Greenwood Press, 1970), Vol. I, 27. Available on line at http://etext.virginia.edu/washington/fitzpatrick (accessed January 19, 2012). Washington further elaborated, "When the fate of America may be at stake on the issue; when the wisdom of cooler moments and the experienced men have decided that we should *protract the war* if possible; I cannot think it safe or wise to adopt a different system." For additional perspective on the evolution of Washington's strategic thinking see, Russell F. Weigley, *The American Way of War; a History of United States Military Strategy and Policy* (New York: Macmillan, 1973), 3-17 and Oliver L. Spaulding, "The Military Studies of George Washington," *The American Historical Review* 29, no. 4 (Jul., 1924): 675-680.

[17] For the development and rationale behind the British Army's emphasis on decisive battle see, Matthew H. Spring, *With Zeal and with Bayonets Only: The British Army on Campaign in North America, 1775-1783* (Norman: University of Oklahoma Press, 2008), 18-23 and Black, *War for America*, 13-40 and 246-247. For the planning, conduct, and missed opportunities of the New York campaign see Ira D. Gruber, *The Howe Brothers and the American Revolution* (New York: Atheneum, 1972), 89-157; Higginbotham, *The War of American Independence*, 148-171; and Mackesy, *The War for America*, 73-102. For a comprehensive and balanced account of the 1777 campaign, perhaps the most crucial year of the war, see, John S. Pancake, *1777, The Year of the Hangman* (University of Alabama Press, 1977). For perspective on the causes and consequences of Saratoga see, Black, *War for America*, 114-145; Higginbotham, *The War of American Independence*, 175-198; Mackesy, *The War for America*, 121-147; and Gruber, *The Howe Brothers*, 173-188.

[18] The global nature of the conflict, from the British perspective, constitutes the dominant theme of Mackesy's critically acclaimed, *The War for America*. See, in particular, pp. 181-186, 262-266, 279-297, 301-318, and 510-518. The larger context of Britain's global responsibilities remains a paramount, if underappreciated, prerequisite for understanding the strategic direction and outcome of the war. Britain's political and military mismanagement of the war in America, however, precipitated the escalation of the conflict into a global war. At times, Mackesy's emphasis on the latter and his interpretation that the loss of America must be placed within the larger context of the war against France, though accurate, appears overly sympathetic if not apologetic. For a more critical interpretation of British strategic failure in America and its implications see, Simms, *Three Victories and a Defeat*, 662-684.

[19] Simms, *Three Victories and a Defeat*, 677.

[20] For insight into the dramatic change in British strategic priorities in the wake of French intervention see, Black, *War for America*, 146-169; Mackesy, *The War for America*, 154-161; and Wilcox, *Portrait of a General*, 211-225.

[21] Black, *War for America*, 151-154. The "terms" the North Ministry empowered Carlisle to make shattered two decades of political intransigence and represented a dramatic and radical reordering of the imperial system. Parliament ceded its right to tax the colonies save for the regulation of trade and granted the Americans direct representation in the House of Commons. In short, it gave the colonists everything they asked for prior to the commencement of hostilities, but withheld the one thing, "open and avowed independence," they declared after the war began. Peace with honor in America, however, fell on deaf ears – a victim to an all too obvious display of British military weakness. The American Secretary, Lord George Germain, coincident

to Carlisle's efforts, ordered Howe's successor, Sir Henry Clinton, to return to New York, detach 5,000 troops for naval operations against St Lucia, and assume a defensive posture on the Hudson if, in the process, Washington's army could not be *destroyed*. Remarkably, in a sign of just how dire the Ministry viewed the situation, Clinton's instructions granted him the discretion to evacuate New York altogether and withdrawal to Halifax, Nova Scotia if the situation so warranted. Though successful, Clinton's subsequent strategic consolidation at New York took on the look and feel of an inglorious retreat to the thousands of loyalists who abandoned their possessions and accompanied his log train to New York or remained behind to meet an uncertain fate at the hands of the Patriots. See, Wilcox, *Portrait of a General*, 229-230 and Mackesy, *The War for America*, 186-189.

[22] Ian Saberton, ed., *The Cornwallis Papers: The Campaigns of 1780 and 1781 in the Southern Theatre of the American Revolutionary War* (East Sussex: Naval & Military Press, Ltd., 2010), Vol. I, 3. Cited hereafter as, *The Cornwallis Papers*. As early as 1777, in the aftermath of Saratoga and the indecision of Germantown, many British politicians were openly considering the abandonment of offensive operations in America in favor of a maritime strategy based on blockade and amphibious raids. See for example, the comments of Basil Feilding, the Earl of Denbigh, and supporter of the North Ministry who, upon leaving London in December 1777 observed that, "all the Kings friends and well wishers to their country in very low spirits indeed; not only on the account of the very extraordinary misfortune that has happened to General Burgoyne, but also on what may happen in consequence… The Cabinet seems very irresolute whether to raise new corps and to carry on the war by land (which in our present situation I think impossible) or to stand upon the defensive in the few places we have got in our hands, or prosecute it vigorously by sea. There is not a foreign soldier more to be got for love or money… We have hitherto kept up our great majority in both houses of Parliament but what will happen when we next meet God only knows." Quoted in Black, War for America, 145. For additional perspective on the erosion of political support in the aftermath of Saratoga see, G.R. Barnes and J.H. Owen, eds., *The Private Papers of John, Earl of Sandwich, First Lord of the Admiralty, 1771-1782* (London: Navy Records Society, 1932-1938), Vol. I, 327-335.

[23] Smith, *Loyalists and Redcoats*, 170-171.

[24] Mackesy, *The War for America,* 237-248. Ironically, the mishandling of British naval policy in the spring of 1778, long a source of imperial strength, produced the most enduring and visible catalyst for strategic and political failure in America. The Admiralty, fearing invasion of the home isles, abandoned its traditional doctrine of blockading French sea power in port in lieu of concentrating the fleet in home waters. When, in the process, De Grasse's fleet broke out, unchallenged, into the open waters of the Atlantic it unleashed a firestorm of political controversy directed at the North Ministry that was exasperated by a very public court-martial of Britain's senior naval officer and Commander of the Channel Fleet, Admiral Augustus Keppel. Also see Smith, *Loyalists and Redcoats* 94-96. For the background and circumstances of General Howe's Parliamentary testimony and subsequent break with the North Ministry, see Gruber, *The Howe Brothers and the American Revolution*, 325-350.

[25] Smith, *Loyalists and Redcoats*, 115-125. For an in-depth examination of the mounting political opposition to the government's policies and conduct of the war see, Herbert Butterfield, *George III, Lord North, and the People, 1779-80* (London: G. Bell and Sons, 1949), 29-35. Butterfield observed, "It is difficult to see what was left for the making of a ministry-difficult to know how such a ramshackle administration can have remained in existence at such a critical time."

[26] Smith, *Loyalists and Redcoats*, 96-99 and 170-171.

[27] For background and context on the government's plans to shift the seat of the war to the Caribbean see, Mackesy, *The War for America*, 225-232. For an early example of the role and influence of the Royal Governors, particularly Josiah Martin of North Carolina, played in exaggerating loyalist strength and shaping military strategy and operations see, Eric Robson, "The Expedition to the Southern Colonies, 1775-1776," *The English Historical Review* 66, no. 261 (Oct., 1951): 538-540.

[28] For the origins and development of Britain's "Southern Strategy" see David K. Wilson, *The Southern Strategy: Britain's Conquest of South Carolina and Georgia, 1775-1780* (Columbia: University of South Carolina Press, 2005), 59-64; Smith, *Loyalists and Redcoats* 113-125; and Mackesy, *The War for America*, 251-256.

[29] Smith, *Loyalists and Redcoats*, 124-125.

[30] Black, *War for America*, 219. Black, in assessing Cornwallis's temperament and conduct of the Southern Campaign, observed: "The earl clearly had no time for pacification, as his later actions in India and Ireland were to show. Instead he continued to seek decisive battle." For a more sympathetic interpretation of Cornwallis and his generalship see, Franklin B. Wickwire and Mary Wickwire, *Cornwallis: The American Adventure* (Boston: Mifflin, 1970), 170-193. For the dysfunctional nature of the North Ministry during this crucial time see Butterfield, *George III, Lord North, and the People, 1779-80* (London: G. Bell and Sons, 1949), 29-35.

[31] Higginbotham, *The War of American Independence*, 356-357.

[32] Ibid., p. 360. Also see, Treacy, *Prelude to Yorktown*, 13-19.

[33] Mackesy, *The War for America, 1775-1783*, 342-345 and Treacy, *Prelude to Yorktown*, 19-27.

[34] "Major Operations in the South, 1780," Source: USMA History Department. Available online at http://www.dean.usma.edu/history/web03/atlases/AtlasesTableOfContents.html (accessed 17 January 2012).

[35] Higginbotham, *The War of American Independence*, 360-363. On May 29, Lt Col Banastre Tarleton's loyalist cavalry ambushed 350 Continentals under the command of Col. Abraham Buford at Waxhaws, near the North Carolina border. According to Patriot accounts large numbers of surrendering Whigs were murdered as they tried to surrender. While the tactical details of the events remain unclear, even to this day, the perception of a British massacre ignited an explosion of visceral hatred that fueled a rapidly burgeoning insurgency.

[36] Treacy, *Prelude to Yorktown*, 20-23.

[37] Weller, "Irregular but Effective," 118-131 and "The Irregular War in the South," 124-136.

[38] Higginbotham, *The War of American Independence*, 364. The "Overmountain Men" resided west of the Great Smoky Mountains in what is today northeastern Tennessee, western North Carolina, and southwestern Virginia. They also fought at the Battle of Cowpens. Largely

of Scotch-Irish descent they established a semi-autonomous government called the Watauga Association in 1772, thus predating the Declaration of Independence by four years.

[39] "Account of Colonel Isaac Shelby," North Carolina State Records XV, 105-108 quoted in Treacy, *Prelude to Yorktown*, 47.

[40] Billias, *George Washington's Opponents*, 122-123; Higginbotham, *The War of American Independence*, 364; Treacy, *Prelude to Yorktown*, 48-53; and Mackesy, *The War for America, 1775-1783*, 344-345.

[41] Greene to Alexander Hamilton, 10 Jan. 1781 in Harold Coffin Syrett and Jacob Ernest Cooke eds., *The Papers of Alexander Hamilton* (New York: Columbia University Press, 1961), Vol. 2, 529-530, quoted in Mark Clodfelter, "Between Virtue and Necessity: Nathanael Greene and the Conduct of Civil-Military Relations in the South, 1780-1782," *Military Affairs* 52, no. 4 (Oct., 1988): 169-175.

[42] Greene to Washington in John Clement Fitzpatrick ed., *The Writings of George Washington from the Original Manuscript Sources 1745-1799*, (Westport, Conn.: Greenwood Press, 1970), Vol. XX, 321, quoted in Treacy, *Prelude to Yorktown*, 58 and 196.

[43] George Washington Greene, *The Life of Nathanael Greene, Major-General in the Army of the Revolution* (Freeport, N.Y.: Books for Libraries Press, 1972), Vol. III, 79-81.

[44] Theodore Thayer, *Nathanael Greene; Strategist of the American Revolution* (New York: Twayne Publishers, 1960), 282-306.

[45] Treacy, *Prelude to Yorktown*, 123.

[46] Higginbotham, *The War of American Independence*, 370.

[47] John S. Pancake, *This Destructive War: The British Campaign in the Carolinas, 1780-1782* (University, AL: University of Alabama Press, 1985), 186. Pancake's work remains the best single volume account of the Southern Campaign. Treacy's, *Prelude to Yorktown* retains enduring value. Both Weigley's, *The Partisan War: The South Carolina Campaign of 1780-1782* and Dederer's, *Making Bricks Without Straw: Nathanael Greene's Southern Campaign and Mao Tse-Tung's Mobile War* are succinct, but exceptionally insightful works. Gordon's, *South Carolina and the American Revolution* combines exceptional prose with judicious content. John Buchanan's, *The Road to Guilford Courthouse: The American Revolution in the Carolinas* (New York: Wiley, 1997) is well researched and offers an outstanding bibliography, but is overly detailed and lacks the penetrating analysis of Pancake or the explanatory power of Weigley or Dederer.

[48] Cornwallis to Clinton, 10 April 1781, *The Cornwallis Papers*, Vol. IV, 110.

[49] Ibid., 11.

[50] Cornwallis to Phillips, 10 April, 1781, *The Cornwallis Papers*, Vol. IV, 115.

[51] Greene to Washington, 29 March, 1781, quoted in Treacy, *Prelude to Yorktown*, 193.

[52] Higginbotham, *The War of American Independence*, 370-374.

[53] Black, *War for America*, 236.

[54] Royal Governor of New York, James Robertson to Lord Amherst, 27 December 1781, quoted in Black, *War for America*, 236.

[55] Ian R Christie, *The End of North's Ministry, 1780-1782* (London: Macmillan, 1958), 267-298 details the political crisis in the immediate aftermath of Yorktown. See pp. 261-266 for the interplay of domestic politics and the planning and conduct of the southern campaign.

[56] William Cobbet, *The Parliamentary History of England*, 36 vols. (London, 1806-1820),Vol. XXII, 1032, quoted in Smith, *Loyalists and Redcoats*, 166-167.

[57] Quoted in Christie, *The End of North's Ministry*, 319-320.

[58] Ibid., 299-369.

[59] Black, *War for America*, 239.

[60] For broader perspectives concerning the root causes of British strategic defeat in America see, John W. Shy, *A People Numerous and Armed: Reflections on the Military Struggle for American Independence* (Ann Arbor, Mich.: University of Michigan Press, 1990), 195-224; Mackesy, *The War for America*, 510-516; William B.Willcox, "British Strategy in America, 1778," *The Journal of Modern History* 19, no. 2 (Jun., 1947): 97-121, *Star of Empire; A Study of Britain as a World Power, 1485-1945* (New York: Knopf, 1950), 156-161, and *Portrait of a General*, 443-444. See also, Smith, *Loyalists and Redcoats*, 168-174; Gruber, "The Origins of British Strategy in the War for American Independence," 41-50; Black, *War for America*, 245-248; Brewer, *The Sinews of Power*, 175-178; and Bowler, *Logistics and the Failure of the British Army in America, 1775-1783*, 239-264.

[61] Black, *War for America*, 219.

[62] Dederer, "Making Bricks without Straw," 115-121.

[63] Higginbotham, *The War of American Independence*, 355 and 363. Also see, Smith, *Loyalists and Redcoats*, 11.

[64] Paul H. Smith, "The American Loyalists: Notes on their Organization and Numerical Strength," *The William and Mary Quarterly* 25, no. 2 (Apr., 1968): 259-277.

[65] Jac Weller, "The Irregular War in the South," 124-136; Weigley, *The Partisan War*, 69-74; and Higginbotham, *The War of American Independence*, 371.

[66] Bowler, *Logistics and the Failure of the British Army in America, 1775-1783*, 89-91.

[67] For additional perspective on the Complex Human Terrain of the Southern Theater as well as the organization, demographics, and development of pre-war Southern society see John Richard Alden, *The South in the Revolution, 1763-1789* (Baton Rouge: Louisiana State University Press, 1957); Edward McCrady, *The History of South Carolina in the Revolution,*

1775-1780 (New York: Russell & Russell, 1969); Richard A. Waterhouse, *New World Gentry: The Making of a Merchant and Planter Class in South Carolina, 1670-1770* (Charleston, SC: History Press, 2005); Saberton, ed., *The Cornwallis Papers*, Vol. 1, 32-35; Weller, "The Irregular War in the South'" 124; and Gordon, *South Carolina and the American Revolution*, 15-19.

[68] For a succinct treatment of Greene and his strategic designs see, Theodore Thayer "Nathanael Greene: Revolutionary War Strategist" in George Athan Billias ed., *George Washington's Opponents: British Generals and Admirals in the American Revolution* (New York: Morrow, 1969), 109-134.

[69] Both Sumter and Pickens violated their original paroles after the British humiliated them and burned their homes see, Treacy, *Prelude to Yorktown*, 20-23 and Weller, "Irregular but Effective," 118-131.

[70] George Washington Greene, *The Life of Nathanael Greene, Major-General in the Army of the Revolution* (Freeport, N.Y.: Books for Libraries Press, 1972), Vol. III, 227.

[71] Shy, *A People Numerous and Armed*, 195-224.

[72] Smith, *Loyalists and Redcoats*, 168-174.

[73] For the dangers inherent in the selective use of historical example see, Micheal Howard, "The Use and Abuse of Military History," in *The Causes of Wars and Other Essays* (Cambridge, Mass.: Harvard University Press, 1984), 188-197. For the preservation of national power see, Richard Haas, "The Restoration Doctrine," *The American Interest* (January/February 2012) available on line at http://www.the-american-interest.com/article.cfm?piece=1164 (accessed 17 February 2012). For both the challenges and consequences associated with America's massive national debt and its likely effects on national defense policy, strategy, and future spending see Donald B. Marron's, "America in the Red," *National Affairs*, (Spring 2010, No. 3): 3-19 and David Barno's, *Hard Choices: Responsible Defense in an Age of Austerity* (Washington, D.C.: Center for a New American Security, 2011).

[74] B.H. Liddell Hart, *The British Way in Warfare* (London: Faber & Faber Ltd., 1932), 11-32.

[75] Brewer, *The Sinews of Power*, 175-178.

[76] Gruber, "The Origins of British Strategy in the War for American Independence," 43. Also see Eric Robson, "The Expedition to the Southern Colonies, 1775-1776." *The English Historical Review* 66, no. 261 (Oct., 1951): 535. Throughout the war the British government consistently struggled to achieve unity of effort across a compartmentalized and non-integrated ministerial system. A fact not lost on Robson who observed, "The practice of each department of government being separate and self-contained, and the minister in charge responsible directly only to the king, rendered the carrying into effect of a vigorous policy more difficult-such a system could not grapple either with the problems of strategy or with those of organization, supply, and transport. The successful execution of plans depended upon an efficiency of organization, and a degree of cooperation between departments, which did not exist-this became visible during the War of American Independence to many of those most deeply concerned."

[77] Harvey to Lt. Gen. Irwin, 230 June 1775, War Office Papers, National Archives, 3/5, folder 37 quoted in Spring, *With Zeal and with Bayonets Only*, 17.

[78] Gruber, "The Origins of British Strategy in the War for American Independence," 42.

[79] J. W. Fortescue, The War of Independence: The British Army in North America, 1775-1783 (London: Macmillan and Co., 1911), 20-22.

[80] Wilson, *The Southern Strategy*, 1-4 and Robson, "The Expedition to the Southern Colonies, 1775-1776," 538-540.

[81] The Earle of Sandwich, First Lord of the Admiralty, quoted in Higginbotham, *The War of American Independence*, 52.

[82] Alden, *General Gage in America*, 218-232 and 234. Beginning in the fall of 1774, Gage repeatedly warned his superiors in London about the growing strength and capability of the rebel movement in America. See Clarence E. Carter ed., *The Correspondence of General Thomas Gage* (New Haven: Yale University Press, 1931), Vol. I, 340-396 and Vol. II, 650-780. See in particular, Gage to Barrington, 2 Nov. 1774, *Gage Correspondence*, Vol. II, 658-659. Gage, writing to Great Britain's Secretary of War, observed: "This Province and the neighboring ones, particularly Connecticut, are preparing for War; if you resist and not yield, that Resistance should be effectual at the beginning. If you think ten Thousand men sufficient, send Twenty, if one million is thought enough, give two; you will save both blood and treasure in the end. A large force will terrify, and engage many to join you, a middling one will encourage resistance, and gain no Friends. The Crisis is indeed an alarming one, & Britain had never more Need of Wisdom, Firmness, and Union than at this Juncture."

[83] Tucker and Hendrickson's *The Fall of the First British Empire: Origins of the War of American Independence* remains the most authoritative treatment of pre-war British policies. See, in particular, pp. 379-410. For additional perspective on the inadequacies and consequences of the British ministerial system during the crucial twelve-year period between the conclusion of the Seven Years War and the outbreak of hostilities in America see Brewer, *The Sinews of Power*, pp. 176-177; Simms, *Three Victories and a Defeat*, 678-683; Wilcox, *Star of Empire*, 157; Gruber, "The Origins of British Strategy in the War for American Independence," 44; Shy, *Toward Lexington*, 418-424; and Ben Baack, "British versus American Interests in Land and the War of American Independence," *Journal of European Economic History* 33, no. 3 (2004): 519-54.

[84] Higginbotham, *The War of American Independence*, 1 and Shy, *A People Numerous and Armed*, 195-224.

[85] Walter Millis, *Arms and Men; A Study in American Military History* (New York: Putnam, 1956), 34-35.

[86] Pancake, *This Destructive War*, 240 and Spring, *With Zeal and with Bayonets Only*, 277-281.

[87] Smith, *Loyalists and Redcoats* pp. 168-174; Spring, *With Zeal and with Bayonets Only*, 277-281; Pancake, *This Destructive War*, 240-244; and Weigley, *The Partisan War*, 1. The basic intellectual dilemma persists today. Weigley, writing nearly forty years ago, ominously

foreshadowed both the nadir of America's tragic involvement in Vietnam and prophetically described the fundamental problem confronting the United States military in the twenty-first century: "The twentieth-century United States has not adjusted easily to involvement in irregular war. Our immense wealth and productivity, our great resources of manpower, and our national conviction that war is an abnormal condition, completely distinct from peace, and a condition which should be terminated quickly in a clear-cut decision, all equipped us admirably to fight and win the two world wars. But they do not fit us so well for limited wars in climate and terrain where massive military power can be in some ways a liability, where victory itself is almost indefinable, and where enemies fight elusively and with methods so thoroughly opposed to conventional rules of war that many of the textbook principles for its conduct are stood on their heads and bring only boomerang results."

[88] For perspective on the irregular nature of warfare in America and the competing philosophies of coercion versus conciliation in the British officer corps see, Conway, "To Subdue America: British Army Officers and the Conduct of the Revolutionary War," 381-407 and Russell, "Redcoats in the Wilderness: British Officers and Irregular Warfare in Europe and America, 1740 to 1760," 629-652.

[89] Smith, *Loyalists and Redcoats* 168-174; Spring, *With Zeal and with Bayonets Only*, 277-281; and Pancake, *This Destructive War*, 240-244.

[90] See, Cornwallis to Phillips, 10 April, 1781, *The Cornwallis Papers*, Vol. IV, 114-115. Cornwallis's frank and candid description of the strategic conundrum confronting the British bears a remarkable similarity to the fundamental dilemma that characterized the United States conduct of the war in Vietnam nearly two hundred years later. For perspective on the U.S. Army's experience in Vietnam see the two competing counterfactual arguments presented in Harry Summers, *On Strategy: A Critical Analysis of the Vietnam War* (Novato, CA: Presidio Press, 1982), 170-173, 181-194 and Andrew F. Krepinevich, *The Army and Vietnam* (Baltimore: Johns Hopkins University Press, 1986), 233 and 268.

[91] Fred Charles Iklé, *Every War Must End* (New York: Columbia University Press, 1971), 1-16. Ikle's well crafted and succinct historical survey serves as a powerful and enduring reminder that the decision to employ force must be taken as part of a realistic and accurate assessment of the enemy's political will, capability to fight, and national risk, vice the short-term expediency of the moment that values hope and ideology over sovereign reason and military reality.

[92] Gruber, "The Origins of British Strategy in the War for American Independence," 41.

[93] For differing perspectives on the future strategic environment see, Colin S. Gray, *Another Bloody Century: Future Warfare* (London: Weidenfeld & Nicolson, 2005), 145-161 and Robert O. Work, "The Future Security Environment: Multidimensional Challenges in a Multi-Player World," Center for Strategic and Budgetary Assessments, August 21, 2008. For future demographics and their likely effects see, Richard Jackson and Neil Howe, *The Graying of the Great Powers: Demography and Geopolitics in the 21st Century* (Washington, D.C.: Center for Strategic and International Studies, May 2008), 5-12.

[94] For informed critiques of the "American way of war" and how it pertains, or fails to pertain, to the contemporary and future operating environments see, Colin Gray, *Irregular Enemies and the Essence of Strategy: Can the American Way of War Adapt?* (Carlisle, PA: Strategic Studies Institute, U.S. Army War College, 2006) and Antulio J. Echevarria, *Toward an American Way of*

War (Carlisle, PA: Strategic Studies Institute, U.S. Army War College, 2004). Echevarria argued that the United States has, in reality, a way of battle, not a true way of war. The British experience in America (1775 -1783), like many contemporary examples of great power involvement in intra-state conflict, suggests caution. The apparent decoupling of traditional military force with the ability to achieve enduring political success plagued the French in Indochina (1946-1954) and Algeria (1954-1962), the United States in Vietnam (1959-1975), the Soviet Union in Afghanistan (1979-1989), the Israelis in Lebanon (1982-2000 and 2006), the Russians in Chechnya (1994-1996), and, at present, threatens the final outcome of America's wars in Iraq and Afghanistan.

[95] Higginbotham, *The War of American Independence*, 127.

Printed in Great Britain
by Amazon